# Baby, Read Me Something with Rhythm

Poems by Carla Christopher

*This volume contains some mature or explicit language and is intended for mature audiences

Copyright © 2012 Carla Christopher

Copyright infringement is bad karma. More specifically, all rights reserved. No part of this book may be reproduced, in any form, without specific permission from the publisher, except by a reviewer who wishes to quote brief passages.

Cover Art by Love Design House & Detroit Royalty
www.krop.com/lovedesignhouse
www.facebook.com/miasimone29
Book Layout and Design by Carla Christopher
Printed in the United States for PoemSugar Press
York, PA      www.poemsugarpress.com
ISBN: 978-0-578-10718-9

## The Poems

| | |
|---|---|
| Poetry Ahead | 9 |
| Consumed (The Book Itself Speaks) | 10 |
| In A Sentimental Mood | 11 |
| Like No Other | 12 |
| We Found Ourselves Here (The Wedding Poem) | 14 |
| Need | 15 |
| Closer | 16 |
| May My Daughter Be Erotic | 17 |
| A Little Like A God | 18 |
| Happiness | 19 |
| 25,480 Hours | 20 |
| Ms. Romeo Day | 21 |
| Sinking Into Rhythm | 22 |
| Q & A | 24 |
| These Breasts of Mine | 25 |
| Spread | 26 |
| When Comes the Goddess | 27 |
| The Haunting | 28 |
| Tonight I Am Sad | 29 |
| Black Widow | 30 |
| My Man | 31 |
| Love Like Creation | 32 |
| Go | 33 |
| Affirmation | 34 |
| Floating On Silence | 35 |
| Write A Letter to Your Father | 36 |
| Rollin' | 37 |
| All the Way Home | 38 |
| Passed On | 40 |
| A Love By Any Other Name | 41 |
| What I Need | 42 |
| God Loves the Blues the Best | 43 |
| The Streets Are A V. | 44 |
| Going Home | 45 |

| | |
|---|---|
| Manhood – A Quartet | 46 |
| One Long Breath (Why I Wouldn't Marry You) | 50 |
| Genealogy | 52 |
| Laced | 53 |
| To My Old Girl | 54 |
| Anything to Fly | 56 |
| Spark | 57 |
| I Wear This Night | 58 |
| Journey | 59 |

*For my family, especially Mama Kate
and for the people in my life who now live inside these poems*


*With gratitude to:
Marcus Colasurdo & The Tribe
The Original Wednesday Emporium Group
The 30/30 Writers; Keith, Crystal, Stefan & Missi
My Sisters of the Pen; Debberae, Rebecca, Christine, Maria
Dana, without whom this book would not be
Mia, for being my artistic muse
and Shaashawn, for the push*

# Baby, Read Me Something With Rhythm

"I write the world I'm waiting for
I write the world I see when I dream
I braid together strands of fantasy
until they are strong enough
to bear the weight of possibility
and then I make the choice to believe"

### Poetry Ahead

Beware!
Poetry ahead
Slippery poetry with dangerous curves
Poetry that demands the right of way
and that cannot stop easily
once things begin charging down hill
This poetry can be difficult to control
It may be best to yield
or even stop
when poetry is in motion
She is known to take
wide left turns
followed by unexpectedly sharp rights
and though the bridge may be icy
you can burn on the before and after
There is no telling where
this poetry is going
so it may be best to yield
or even stop
when poetry is in motion

### Consumed (The Book Itself Speaks)

Read me to you lover
Go on, spread me open
Lift page from page
and lay me against her stomach

Touch her while you read
Not so fast my dear
Be absent-minded at first
Turn your fingertips to feathers
and trace the curves of where
her wings would be

Very good, now
tread softly, but with purpose
Like the huntress,
corner your prey
and know that she is yours

The fire in your eyes begins to smolder now
Let the sparks fly out into
the receptive tinder of her hair
Let me lay in ashes,
forgotten and
consumed

### *In A Sentimental Mood*

When I met you it was dissonance
I admit it, I kept my distance
dancing in and out of tune
You were a new thing

and I play a solo gig
pausing for brief moments of collaboration
but always with a moment of
      hesitation
before I dive in and swim
Improvisation is not my thing

Do you have this written down somewhere?
The music is pouring in my ear
when you speak and spilling over
down my cheek like rain
or come shine
making me enjoy this thing

Switching keys
I just got a little bit
      higher
Hold on, I'm feeling this
I'm gonna ride this note
play with it a moment
then draw it out 'til blue skies
and summertime

### *Like No Other*

Others have loved you
for your almond eyes
and cocoa skin and hips
that move like delicious sin incarnate
but I could exist in blissful starvation
surviving only on the airy meringue of your kiss
sipping the wild berry of your lips
licking even at the salt of your sarcasm,
without growing thirsty

Others have loved you
for the artistic merit of your show
the music your magical fingers perform,
the muscular thrust
of your clever dancing thighs
but I train you for
the acrobatic arch of your back
when I push you into involuntary motion,
the tremble and flex of your fists
that clench without rhythm
trying to find something solid in air
so thick with tension
you could glide slick against it
and find satisfaction

Others have loved you
in fractured numbers
and across experiential spectrums,
the crystal brilliance of your body
splitting white light good intentions
into rainbows sliding
brilliantly downward into magically delicious
rain soaked arcs of desire,
each lover another color

*but I will wait for you in darkness,*
*find you by scent alone,*
*map the goose bumps on your skin and find the pictures*
*within them like constellations on a moonless night,*
*then I'll make love before sunrise*
*to the shapes I find between the stars*

### *We Found Ourselves Here (The Wedding Poem)*

*We*
*of our two separate names like*
*opposite ends of a rainbow spectrum*
*remember that any two colors*
*are born of the same light*
*when we come together*
*Broken down for human eyes*
*the beauty of our bodies assembled illuminates*
*the complexities of two lives*
*twisted braided loc'ed*
*into one representation of growing strength*
*Wholeness in invisible union*
*bringing soul salvation*
*to those creating a place*
*where one voice*
*will always say*
*"I got you, no... we got us"*
*Your passion and power are patterns in light*
*I memorized upon loving you*
*Our hands joined*
*so that even in darkness*
*we find each other as irrefutable reality*
*until we begin*
*in another life*
*and find ourselves here*
*again*

## Need

I'm not stealing, I'm sampling
I'm borrowing the feel of your space
and getting the kisses for free
It's like roomies
Like cellies
Like sorority sisters
I'm just making the best
of the universe putting us in time together
Did I say this all out loud?
My tongue must be satin sheet slippery
'cause I can't hold it
No wonder you like it when I go down so much
I'm still working on my
apologetic confession
because I did snatch a mouthful
in a moment of need
but if a soul is suffering from starvation
is a crumb a crime?
In fact, I think you should share with me
as a testimonial to your generosity
and I will be
no longer a thief but rather, actively
grateful

**Closer**

You wrap around me
like old fashioned curling telephone wire
and from your voice
to my ear
with you there and me here
I can feel the physical
completion I seek in our
coupling when I grasp
squeeze you until you pop
Your insides
meeting my outsides
and I can lick you off
Take you inside
my open mouth
my guts touching
more than I can grab
in two dimensions

### *May My Daughter Be Erotic*

My Mama rocks notes like an orchestra
symphonic seduction
tumbling out over rolling hill lips
pooling between the
curving valleys that are her
hips
I slid out on a rainbow
awash with salty juices that
made me a mermaid
A natural born fisher
of women
of men
There is nothing better
then the legacy of voodoo goddess rising
Grandmother to Mother and
Mother to Daughter
My sweet young thing
May the apple be rich
and not far from the tree
the nectar, a cooling slide
between the unfurling buds of your breasts

**A Little Like A God**

How I would love to have created you
to have reached out my hand
and raised you from the dust
to have knitted together the form of your body
and sculpted the clay of your soul
to have breathed the fire that hardened you

to have, with a kiss's press,
put vision in your eyes
and be the first to experience your touch
to know you could never leave me
a part of you belonging to
the sunlight and loam
that daily touch my naked skin

I've never wanted to be a deity
For me such power holds no allure
but oh, to have created you
would be enough to change
a woman's mind

*Happiness*

Woke up this mornin' with the taste
of last night's confidences still on my breath
Makes me want to let my teeth go a day or so
Let that sweet freedom roll around
where it ain't used to being
Tasting those sweet little happinesses
like nothing the boss got to say gonna
get to me today
Twist my tongue around the happiness
that ran so thick I can still taste it
sliding sweet down my throat in slow molten rivers
beneath the ground of hilly curves
erupt like lava
where I open
and you explore inside
Car can't hit me
Man on the street words bounce off me
like school yard chants
I can be the rubber
if you will be the glue that holds me together
and keeps me with you
I go off to work with a jaunt in my step
'cause he and she and she don't know
what I know
about what you can do

## 25,480 hours

So the question is, "Do you want to sex with me?"
Not "Do you want to have sex?"
The question is do you want muscle tight rope tension wire
I am alive more in this 1 hour
then in the 97,464 hours I will spend
(so They say) at work ?
As the statistical poster child that I am
I only have 25,480 hours for hair tangling
sweaty red mark neck biting
feral claw shoulder catching wordlessly telling you
that I'm begging
So that's why this isn't just about sex
Sex with me involves kissing
Tongue tracing lip outlines
and hovering over the sexy top lip dip
my tongue your tongue cuddling before
foreshadow thrusting 'our kisses are kissing each other' kissing
Sex with me is grinding reach behinds
to feel the outline of what's warming and
well on it's way to a simmering slow burn of arousal
Let me season and soften all day
until the aroma hangs in the house
like a soft and spicy olfactory overlay
Sex with me falls apart on your tongue when your mouth
takes that first bite
and if the sheets are still on the bed
we have not finalized the arrangement of limbs
into a pose of replete exhaustion from
moments devoured and sucked down
to bone and softened skin
So the question is not just are you here just to have sex
but, are you here to have sex with me?

**Ms. Romeo Day**

*I got a rise out the morning
and I'm cruising straight into a
baby blue afternoon, color
of the blanket your voice snuggles me
into. Inside you
is where the morning feels like it is,
where I feel like I am, so
when the outside wonders at some
crazy happy humming I just
keep on moving –
toward a midnight afternoon of
deep blue and exploding stars
I grab by the tail and wrestle down filled
with new energy and
ride the night.
Another wild woman with a
twisted tongue
tangling into yours with
abandon under the cool blue dome
of night.*

### Sinking Into Rhythm

i found the beat
i dun' finally found the beat
and now i'm sinking
into a rhythm
that's drowning me and hitting
somewhere above the ears
so my eyes can just
barely peer over the edge
and i'm seein' you
each wave lapping like a sound
with a beat that makes sense
a series come together
when everything else comes apart
scattered by the vibration
what falls away
meant to go

i got no time
cause i'm dancing in water now
making waves start to spin
a sucking tidal pulling us together
chest to chest
my face turned up toward sun
my arms rise up out of the wet
to the warm

i am oshun bathed in beauty
and my hair is beautiful
my skin is beautiful
i reflect the sun with skin
of glass and mirror
and my rhythm is all of creation

the embodiment of She

*everything
this beat was meant to be
and i am dancing*

*happy*

## Q & A

Can you share a therapist with someone you are dating?
> Answer – not if the therapist thinks the person you are dating is hot. In that case, be highly suspicious of recommendations for separate therapy sessions

Can you share a fuck buddy with a friend?
> Not simultaneously

Can you keep a friend when you discover you have the same fuck buddy over dinner?
> Answer – Not if you are on a diet. You'll be there talking for a while and will end up ordering dessert.

Can you have a friend who is also a former lover?
> Absolutely. Except for the highly probable intoxication induced bar hook up weekend that occurs right after the break-up. And the three weeks of additional whoring after you get your first internet dating site hits. And the first time you see your ex-lover out with your replacement. It doesn't really matter who she is. You can be friends with your ex and the girl AFTER the girl after you, but never with the girl right after you. Unless she is your ex too. You can only lose so much of your friendship circle at one time.

Who should you turn to for relationship advice?
> Not your mother. She's probably right, but you won't listen. Daytime talk shows at this point can be helpful. You really *did* know in the first three months why your three year relationship was eventually going to end in a rubble of disaster and resentment. I would highly recommend a couple who is in a relationship you would actually want to be in. You have to find one first.

What about the important questions not motivated by sex, love or indulgent alcoholic musings?
> There aren't any.

### These Breasts of Mine

Thank you ancestors for these breasts
that have earned me free coffee
and a place in line closer to the ticket window
than my running late rights
should have granted me
That make art from a V neck
and rescue little black dresses
from visual obscurity
Thank you mother
for these breasts
that forced me to arch my back
and toss up my chin
to counter balance their weight
That gave me a strut walk
head high and back straight
and made men hold open doors
to dirty looks from their women
only my breasts don't believe in competition
We can take on all these men together
Thank you creator
for breasts that play well with the curves
of my striding length legs and capable shoulders
I am a landscape in pairs
My symmetry and order a testament
to your perfect plan demanding I acknowledge
these breasts are outstanding

## *Spread*

Running my fingers through your hair
the motion catches
and scatters the light
I cup it in the palm of my hand
and wipe it across my body

In my mind you glow
the night spread behind you
creamy and thick
like peanut butter

### When Comes the Goddess

A vision of beauty
seats herself upon a lotus
enfolded in the scented caress of it's center
An instrument of song
nested between her breasts
a bird awaiting song
rhythmically caressed
by the soft skills of her fingers
so mother tender
I would give you the title of goddess
were it not already yours
and were it mine to give

### The Haunting

i'll just sit here and not bother you
occupied
by the straining underneath my shirt
heart twisting inside my chest
like to burstin'

if i died like this
i would spend the rest of my life
haunting you

**Tonight I Am Sad**

Tonight I am sad
I allow myself to express this
simplicity of emotion
The combination of hunger
fatigue
and the remembrance of fear
I seek stillness
The filling of myself with bread and water
The reassurance of human touch
Please touch me
Smooth me with your hands
and comfort me with your kisses
Join me in my silence
but not my sadness
I go there alone

### Black Widow

please baby let me
raze my tongue over all your wounds
lioness curl myself around you
and rasp away the scar tissue
ripping it down to blood and tender skin again
so that you can feel me
with my sandpaper mother's tongue

let me flip you over with the force
of how badly I want to take care of you
hold you down and hot brand you
so that you don't get lost
when you wander away
as you are wont to do

let me sink my fangs into you
seep sweet numbing poison into your blood
that you never feel pain
paralyze you, so you will never be lured into
what could ensnare you
tie you down enmesh you
in my web but to save you
always to save you   us   my own self

if I had to choose
it would be the one I love the most
and so I would lay bait for you
and hold you
and lose you
to keep you ... still

**My Man**

We collide
Your soul sees my body
and slides into me
like Jackie Robinson
on a pop fly home run
that keeps 'em coming
Leaping in the aisles
on their knees in a hallelujah
crying Amen Yes, Sir
That's my baby
mmhmm, that is *my* man

Like a fish out the water
you break through my placental barrier
because the cosmic clock
chimed the time of arrival
was right on
and you're a born fighter
I cry on my knees
Hallelujah
'cause to make it in this world
you're gonna need more strength
than just my love can give you

**Love Like Creation**

Your smile washes over me like milky way
star shine Like divine
intervention breaking through
the hazy shade of winterfall
Skies make me forget
beneath the heat
of a dark blue and green blanket
I sweat with purifying exhaustion
Your loving has laid me bare
to feel the scratch against my skin   Raw
emotion filling me to the point of satiation
but I can never get enough –
And that's when you come to me
Kiss me quiet
Your tongue swirling in slow circles   You hypnotize
me   The love in your eyes
making me your willing captive
wrapped deep in the silky black sheath of
another night    I whisper
you are my reason
My reason for everything

## Go

Tawny gold
Tanned
Strung-out
Too much sun, no block
No barriers
No roots to soak up the
Blue and Black
Blood and Water
moving through
mixing in my side
down my body
in academic courses
See myself in the pool at my feet
Eroding
Slipping down my own banks
Tumbling over the edges into the
Blue Blue Water
to the tune of Resurrection Gospel
and it's cool
deep and sweet and happy too
I feel Black angels singing
musical moans that dip and swell
The rising and falling
of Deep Mother River
bumping me sweet baby home
carrying me straight into that
sugar yellow sun
Laughing through a mouthful of water
we can catch the flow
and go and go and go

**Affirmation**

I am the beat
that set the rhythm
That got the song on its feet
and made him dance
I am constantly becoming
Drumming
The pulse that opens the doors
and let's God's songs come spinning out
from between my teeth
my lips, my hips
knocking back and forth like
rainbow spreading maracas
As Maya says
If I had known better
I would have done better
But I am the best that I can be
in this now
in this moment
in my rhythm
as I give it wings
and cut it free

**Floating On Silence**

Many river legs
from under Mami Water swollen bellies
and open river mouths
make crosses
on the landscape of my pathless travel and
I am most lovely rain plastered
and water painted
I see in flashes of sky and star and waves until
both are somersault streak tumbles of black that sing
for my listening because to open my mouth here
is to drown
to go down sleepily, slowly
and dream unendingly
yet the gentleness of that hand
placed across my lips
provokes only my kiss
and my drift
floating on silence

## Write A Letter to Your Father

Write a letter to your father
Black Woman
and tell him how you feel
Turned to sister love
the smell of sandalwood and roses
and the wide swing of the woman's arm
as she casts her cracked seed
bread crusts
to the birds
It is no waste to her

I see the woman bent over
her cello belly, violin breasts gently strumming
each other as they sway back and forth
She is the bass

There is no room for you here
Black Father
which is why she built these walls
Your outline is the darkness
in her window glass eyes
Your emptiness
makes room for the echo
of her music

*Rollin'*

*People tell me I walk
like the kind of girl who only wants one thing
but I just laugh and say, it's okay
I got everything that I need*

*People tell me I got a little too much flash
in my swishin' sashay
but nothin' they say don't roll off like candy
me bein' slick as fresh tongued sugar beads
and sweet as can be*

*'Cause people tell me they heard news spillin out
and ain't it lucky they caught those words
before they rolled right out the door?*

*But I just turn my head
'cause I got other things to listen to
Like my sweet baby's laugh
risin' high above kitchen water and cat's meow*

*Oh I know people talk
They do all the things
they feel they got to do
But I just let it roll
'cause they all still outside
and I'm in here rollin' with you*

### All the Way Home

I've realized how indistinctive
the human face becomes if you look at it
long enough
and how beautiful
the human face becomes if you look at it
close enough
and that perfume is a terrible thing to do
to another commuter
and that t-shirt slogans are never as witty as they should be
and the people
*the millions and millions of people*
I feel like they are **all** riding my route.

Ride cause they broke -
saving creation
and the nation
was not a part of their choice
on how to get from A to B
living from Friday to Friday
and Paycheck to Paycheck - I've learned
the meaning of the modern day twist
Wage Slave.

I've learned that there are too many cell phones
and that pretty girls almost always look unhappy
and that no matter what color your skin is...
lime green is not a color you skin was meant to be wearing...
and that pink rollers are a never ending fashion statement
in the land of ghetto fabulous.

I've realized how few people there are
that are actually the person my mother wanted me to be
*that I am not -*

*goes without saying* but somehow you thought
that getting all those women back into a
respectable workplace
was better than them waiting for
the respectable life that they were waiting for
only Life
is a word you don't hear much unless you're in a car
then it's *my* car
and *my* passengers and *my* way
that people violate and force me to use *my* horn -
I don't choose who sits next to me
in metro station seething like Calcutta but
with Christians
on an adventure in the field crying
*wee wee wee wee all the way home*…

I've realized how indistinctive
the human face becomes if you look at it
long enough
and how beautiful
the human face becomes if you look at it
close enough
and that perfume is a terrible thing to do
to another commuter and that
t-shirt slogans are never as witty as they should be
and the people
*the millions and millions of people*
I feel like they are *all* riding my route.

**Passed On**

I have my mother's eyes
and at times I think
I feel the thrill
of her madness
which turned routine
into chase
and rest into
oblivion
I have my father's hands
and in their grip
is the assured and careful strength
which can upend tables
chairs
and smaller people
than I, with my grandfather's
stocky frame

## *A Love By Any Other Name*

Come with me Mahal Kita[1]
to the land behind my eyes, ripe and juicy
with overflowing sunrises of grapefruit pinks
and dreamy sweet-tart purples
where birds trill in harmony and their notes
twist lyrically into symphonic destiny
Yes, these notes were *meant* to sing together
And we were meant to be here
crying diamond tears and collecting
the opalescent crystals into velvet bags
where they jingle
to only the right music, habeeb[2]
Here we swim in pools of pearls and paint in poetry
using words of brightest colors grown in
crumbling rich soil
We grind glimmering shells
into pigments that don't dye
but live alive and breathe on the page and
all my poetry is your beautiful name
whispered into woven parchment
mon amor, tu amada[3]

---

[1]  Tagalog - "Beloved"
[2]  Arabic - "My Love"
[3]  Spanish - "My love, you are loved"

## *What I Need*

Tonight I need to feel your love
need it to press it's feet on the small of my back
I need to arch my spine over it
clench my fists and brace my jaw
against crying out loud as the jar of it rattles my teeth
I need to have the breath pushed out of me
your love a corset fist

I need Lips Fingertips Teeth
to smack and bump when we kiss
fall into each other
hit walls and roll through
I need your knuckles to white and your hair to curl
and I need to know that you're on fire down there

I need to see you crawl
I need your muscles to ripple
shudder and sway like saplings in a gale storm
I need to look at you and remember when
human was animal

My memory was never that good
and I hate to waste it thinking on
when last you made me feel a predatory thrill
because I wore a skirt that showed my thigh

Mostly baby, I need you
and I don't want to get used to not getting'
Cause one way or another
what I need I got to have

**God Loves the Blues the Best**

God obviously loves the Blues the best
He put that much of it in this world
and kept it high or wet
which most people agree
are two of the best states of being
He placed the Blues where man couldn't discolor them
but we still found our way to leave dark trails
of silence and stillness
that marked "we were here"

You leave blue on me
when you paint handprint shaped butterflies on my ass
and every bride hides her hint of blue
beneath shiny light breaking white
It reminds her that no matter how good it gets,
you'll always be a little bit blue once the "y"
comes off the front of "your" dreams and leaves
just the "our".

If angry is red and jealous is green
no wonder the holidays are fucked
and I'm stuck reaching for the golden ring
but falling back into black
where I have managed to travel lightly and infrequently
I know I've see you before
in that place everyone who feels has made a visit to
or called home or at least blown through
I'm pretty sure we've all spent some time
singing the Blues

### The Streets Are a Vampire

If vampires are awake in the sun
when do we sharpen our knives?
If the metal toothed beast never stops feeding
when do we eat and grow strong?
When can mothers safely take phone calls?

    One or two clock changes ago
    I called myself a teacher in this city
    preaching devotion and discovery
    of yesterday's urban poetry to
    today's urban spitters until he –
    the one with guitar playing
    chin cupping before kissing hands –
    he drew a gun on the back of his copy
    of Langston Hughes "Mother to Son"

    He knew enough to turn it over
    when I started making my way from the front
    but he also knew enough
    to put detail on the hammer
    and the slide  stop  grip  safety
    Yes, I met a gun or two
    I used to sleep in the backs of pick ups
    and walk the tunnels on the subway tracks
    and of course my mama feared ringing phones
    and late night shuffle footed door knocks
    but I still had enough blood in me to make it home

**Going Home**

Morning muffin
Oven fresh or day old rescue
don't matter
like the names of the bleeding berries
Blue black (-er, sweeter juice) red
no, rasberry
Razzing like kids
street corner hip and
playing the dozens
'til we crack like fresh eggs
Hard like shell
Tender like shell
Toss in an extra for the baker
there's room on the stoop
creating like God
No one keeps track of the numbers
except God and Mama
from "g'night baby"
to "mornin' muffin"

### *Manhood - Poem One*

My cousin lost her little man
to a big man
that was supposed to be a father man
a There Man
a Caring Man
But he turned out to be an impatient man
with too big a hand that crushed a cry back into
Silence...
That...
S-t-r-e-t-c-h-e-s...
And the pain still hits
like aftershocks from an earthquake that
Just
Won't
Die

### Manhood - Poem Two

I gotta man
that makes my mama's eyes
flash like bomb threats
as memories go off in her head

I don't even remember the Daddy Man
that made Mama ration out love
like war time gasoline
so I didn't know to recognize
smooth enemy lines

I learned that smoky women voices
and flammable breath
both own the territory of the unknown
late night
and that the smell of lies and liquor
hasn't changed in 20 years

It's a cocktail of flat busted 40s
and a shot of women's tears
then add a twist of sour lime
to the wrinkle in time
that laid my mother's life
on top of mine

## Manhood - Poem Three

My brother knows
he's not the man he should be
but he left the Man in Iraq
and just the Hood came home
He wanted to be
unbreakable plastic in clean army green
but when he looks at me
all he hears are the screams
echoing...

So play on playa
caking your face with
pain dulling powder
like suffocating mouthfuls of
hot desert sand
To know a fight ain't right
don't make you less of a man

## Manhood - Poem Four

See, my homegirl
says she should'a been born a boy
But now he defines his days
in the absence of joy when a man heart
beats woman's blood
through a hated chest
each breath pressed
against an invisible wall
bound inside a body prison
a solitary confinement that
cannot even let itself in
devouring the man
inside you *that feels so Real*

Like a snake consuming it's rattling tail
stilling motion with fangs steeped in poison
a warrior's body is his greatest weapon
but a weapon turned upon the body that wields it
can cause the greatest destruction
landing us once more
in s-i-l-e-n-c-e.

**One Long Breath (Why I Wouldn't Marry You)**

Inhale...

Smooth swagga
and kisses so slick
you make me think
/pulled them from *you*
We alternate push and pull
in a tidal struggle
Power shifting like sand
draining from the man in the moon's
clench fisted hand
but onto the shores of the mother land
Oceans I've never seen
lands I've never mapped
or ascribed ownership to
like I laid claim to you
when you dangled another bitch
before me like catnip
Made me roll over
and bare my belly
The softness I so rarely let you see
but your promises demanded nothing less of me
than eternity, child bearing and matrimony
and waiting
for just that right moment when fate and stars and
cash flow would all fall together
and let you make an honest woman of me
Honestly,
my honesty with me
is what kept me waiting on you
masturbating just over faded photos of you
but never pushing you to make those lies true
because I love the way you lie
far better than the way you made me cry

and pay rent when your change was spent
pushing harder and harder against the finish line
of what it would take
for me to be finished
watching your solid body ooze poison smoke
until you didn't know if you were coming up
or going down
I let myself be slain
by your weapons grade apology
like a Buddha with lives to spare
dying from my
compassion
Promising every time
was one time away from the last time
the ringfree nakedness of that
*I am a completed woman* finger
was the only thing that let me believe
that I was waiting for something
because that I was already there
was more truth
than I had the strength to bare...

... and exhale

*Genealogy*

I am the ocean and the sky and the sea
and God in Her infinite wisdom
Oh My God
Oh My God
Oh My God, why hast though forsaken
and in Her infinite wisdom God made
Me
Brown-gold cougar colored woman
with the colors of the world
shining on my tanned hide like a movie
starring Cleopatra, Queen of the Nile
as "The Amiable Consort" in a dramatic
cameo just before her time was called, her
name lost in ages, now a listing
consisting of "Unknown Slave Woman"
hammered deep, deep, deep in stone
My picture is grainy
chopped into pieces of
black and white transmission
worn and cracked one, two
in search of
restoration
Hush baby, don' cry
My cougar colored memories rise
like incense
and wrap you in the tale of
a sweet, sweet
lullaby

***Laced***

Similar goals laced with similar dreams
create two sprits joined at the seams
who become
seamless

Lyric and melody
play as separate song speeches that weave into
counterpoint harmony
two strands stronger together
We pull without splitting

Because we are well made
a spiritual creation
from a spiral of origin energy
that births chaos and beauty
we become bigger

than you and bigger than me
You make me see beauty
condensation on this bar glass
reminding me of the Caribbean sea
drops sparkling like jewelry
I want you to adorn yourself with me
wear me draped across your curves proudly
your prized possession
still allowed to run free

## To My Old Girl

I know it's not your main disease
but the symptomatic flow of lies
coming from the slash of sickness that is
your mouth
is problematic to my
peace of mind and I can't cuddle
in the comfort of cold snow cocaine.
*Sure, you make it rain*
but, like piss, it just drains away
and what do you have to show?

I'm just jumpy,
thinking those sounds that go bump in the night
are really you hitting the door.
At the slightest noise
I have both feet on the floor but
I'm only in time to see you roll down the street.
I caught that last floorboard creak and I sleep
with the keys in my pocket now but
I forgot you have feet too
and before I can say
"what's love got to do with it"
you're gone...

and I can't keep up with your manic pace,
I don't self-medicate the way you do.
Then again, I've never had to go through
the funhouse of demons
haunted by midnight clowns injecting their semen into
little girls    lost    and    wandering    but
even in a maze where the walls are alive with
unwanted hands fondling in the darkness,
You Have Choices.

*Yes, the stories you told gave new definitions to
my worst case scenario
but if only one of us
can get off this island then baby, I'm taking the boat.
I have to go.*

**Anything To Fly**

Gimme a beat Lord
and free my soul
I wanna get lost
and go and go and go

Do you ever just wish
that angels and demons weren't just
elaborate schemas with color palates ranging
from dark to light?
Both sides are capable of flight and
frankly, I would fly with either side –
reach out my hands and trace
the body curves of Dawn,
let land be a horizontal footnote to the tale of
My Escape

Supposing the opposing bookends of our
human mediocrity
could elevate by proximity –
I would gladly volunteer my services
in the systematic testing of the speed of light
versus the speed of darkness
I consider myself an equal opportunity
employer of proactive escapist technology

I just wanna fly

**Spark**

I brush against you
and a certain static activates
causing flesh to cling to flesh
long enough to crackle
an awareness of magnetic
catch
I use caution
in the heat generated
by the friction but
I want to strike you
to see if we spark

## *I Wear This Night*

From my little girl beginning
I saw sweetened cream and satin in the moonlight
Mermaids swam beneath my bath waters
Stars winked in secret code
and played peek-a-boo beneath cloud covers
Spring trees unfolded themselves like ballerinas
and I wanted a tutu of their pink blossoms

Tonight I wear the rose gold
of the street lamp outside our bedroom window
textured and heavy through old glass
repurposed and reframed
light solid as metal
linked in draping ropes across my neck
bare breasts
and a hand
palm up against summer heated sheets

I only sing to let the cats know I am home
and because my grandmother says
it will keep my houseplants from dying
but there was something on the radio tonight
that I wrapped myself in before I left the house
because it rubbed on me silky
and kept getting caught in that magic place between my thighs
so I keep humming a little
now and then to keep it from falling off
and leaving me naked
wearing only the night

## *Journey*

My path is lined with bodies
women who laid themselves down
stacked like cord wood
ridges of flesh my ladder
and I am rising, rising
like a mountain from the hill studded horizon
like passion in an open mouth kiss
shaken to life by the shock of electric
energy that has only changed form
I will document my journey
and on my death
I will leave a map

# About the Author

Carla Juliana Christopher had gypsy beginnings leading her from North Carolina missionary compounds to Detroit housing projects. An Ivy League educated social worker by trade, she has also sung, sketched, acted, stage managed, and written her way across most of the Midwest and East Coast and is the 4th Poet Laureate of York, PA. "Jules" currently lives a sensual, fun-filled life surrounded by indulgent friends, spoiled rescue animals and Wonder Women collectibles in Pennsylvania.
Check her out on the web at:
http://www.facebook.com/PoetryWarriorCarla

**Other Books by Carla Christopher**
Addicted to Relapse (PoemSugar Press/2013)
Song (Columbia University Press/out of print)

# Acknowledgements

This book was produced with much gratitude to The Almost Uptown Poetry Cartel (Harrisburg, PA), Ragged Edge Poetry (Gettysburg, PA), Convergence @ The Readers Café (Hanover, PA), The Parliament, (York, PA), Poetry Spoken Here @ Borders Bookstore (York, PA), Benevolent Armchair @ YorkArts (York, PA), The York Emporium Bookstore and their gracious hosts; Marty Esworthy, Christine O'Leary Rockey, Dana Sauers, Rich Hemmings, Missi Mclaren, Carol Clark-Williams, Barbara DeCeasre, & Jim Lewin.

Great appreciation also goes out to the book's first reader and editor, Missi McLaren, and to model/artist/graphic designer Mia Simone of Detroit Royalty.

www.ingramcontent.com/pod-product-compliance
Lightning Source LLC
Chambersburg PA
CBHW060430050426
42449CB00009B/2224